ZAGG & THE PLANETARY DEFENDERS!

ZAGG and the PLANETARY DEFENDERS

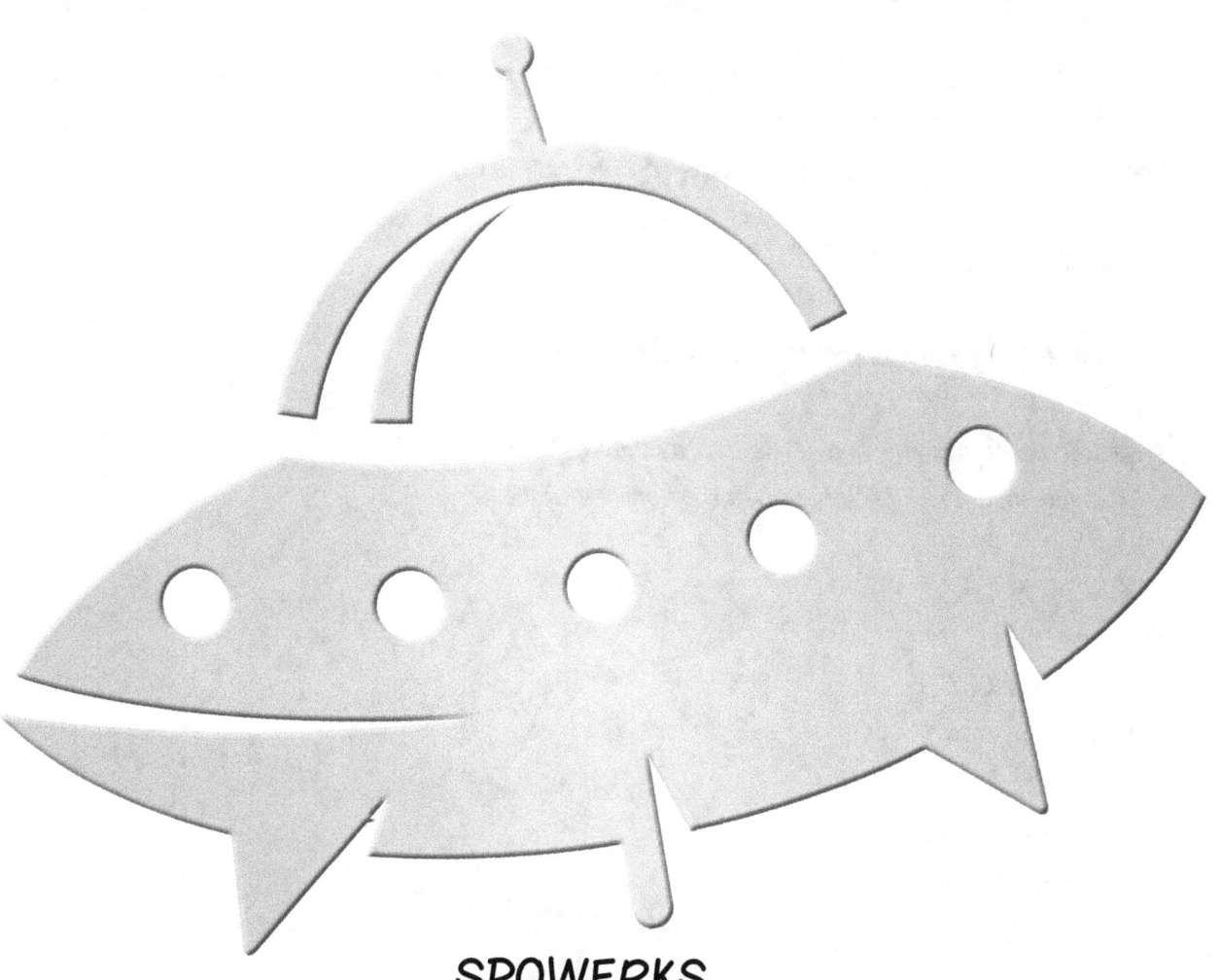

SPOWERKS
- Storyboard -
2018

©2018, Spowerks Storyboard

All rights reserved. This book or any portion thereof may not be reproduced or used in any manner whatsoever without the express written permission of the publisher except for the use of brief quotations in a book review or scholarly journal.

ISBN: 978-1-73256-170-0

Library of Congress Control Number: 2018952659

Available online at www.spowerks.com, as well as from
Lulu, Amazon, Barnes & Noble and other online retailers.

SPOWERKS
P.O. Box 23
Columbia, CT 06237
www.spowerks.com

Printed in the U.S.A.

Dear Adult,

I have written this book because I believe in the mission of Spowerks Storyboard: to explore imagination and creativity through storytelling and art. We do this through:

- character-driven storybooks that engage readers as illustrators
- workshops for students
- educational blog posts and videos
- social media prompts for parents

With this book, I have written the story, and the children are tasked with creating the illustrations. They will need your help. I have included some resources at the back of this book for you to use, but more importantly, just be with them while they are working. Read to them. Listen to them. Encourage them. Give them feedback.

As a former teacher, and as a parent, I am always looking for ways to engage my kids and share something together, something we can be proud of. Completing this book will be a positive and rewarding experience.

This is an opportunity to have kids interact with text, have fun, and be creative. Thank you for your purchase and have fun!

Sincerely,

C.S. Moon, Author

Dear Reader:

Hello! This book is a series of poems, vignettes, and descriptive paragraphs designed to tell the story of Zagg, a pilot who lives on the planet Zorax, and his quest to stop the evil Dr. Zenith and his powerful robot dinosaur.

The story is written and you create the illustrations! Wherever you see a blank page, read the suggestion at the bottom, and draw your own picture!

There are some blank illustration pages at the back, too. Use them if you want to draw other things or if you make a mistake. (Simply cut out the page, redo your drawing, and glue it over the original).

I hope this book is unlike anything you have read before. Have fun, work hard, and let your imagination run free!

Enjoy!

C.S. Moon, Author

THIS BOOK

Welcome creator, to this extraordinary book.

There's lots to discover so take a close look.

It's a story of a hero on a dangerous quest,

because these are stories we all love best.

The poems are written, as you can see;

it needs the illustrations,

so let your imagination run free.

START BY CREATING YOUR OWN COVER FOR THE BOOK ⟶

ZAGG and the PLANETARY DEFENDERS

WRITTEN BY C.S. MOON

Illustrated by

THE PLANET ZORAX

Beyond the shadows of space is a peaceful little planet called Zorax. It has large green deserts, deep oceans of silvery liquid, and large towering cities. It is run by President Zanthos of the Zenton Sector, and kept safe by an army called the Planetary Defenders.

A few years ago, Zorax was attacked by an alien race of sand worms, known as the Nightcrawlers! They descended on Zorax to take over Zulu, the planet's largest, hottest desert. They were merciless invaders who destroyed many of the towns and cities of Zorax.

They almost won the war, if not for the heroic Planetary Defenders and their champion — a courageous pilot named Zagg and his trusty spaceship Rosie.

With Rosie's help, Zagg single-handedly destroyed the leader of the Nightcrawlers, a blubberous mass of undulating flesh named Wormses-Burrower of Death! It cost Zagg an eye, but Wormses' defeat sent the Nightcrawlers racing back to the cold depths of space.

All has been quiet since their defeat, but today that will change. An evil physicist named Dr. Zenith, fired from his job as the Planetary Defenders' chief scientist by President Zanthos, has decided he wants to rule Zorax.

The Defenders have gotten soft over the years. Will they be able to stop his evil plot?

DRAW A PICTURE OF PLANET ZORAX AS SEEN FROM SPACE!

THE PLANETARY DEFENDERS
(THE ARMY THAT DEFENDS PLANET ZORAX)

When planet Zorax is threatened, who will be there?

The Planetary Defenders!

Who commands the land, sea, and air?

The Planetary Defenders!

When all else fails who will dare?

The Planetary Defenders!

Who engages the enemy with an icy stare?

Who puts the planet in their care?

The time is now! Get off that chair!

It's time to join

The Planetary Defenders!

DRAW A PICTURE OF THE PLANETARY DEFENDERS FLAG OR CREST

ZAGG

Eye patch

Purple skin

Pointed tail

Pilot

Soldier

Warrior

Dressed in black

Their last hope

DRAW A PICTURE OF ZAGG

ROSIE

What's that sound way up high?

A streak of lightning across the sky?

Oval shape, cockpit dome,

She always brings Zagg back home.

Thrusters GO!

Cannons FIRE!

Rosie spells the enemy's doom —

With a spin and a twist and a sonic

BOOM!

DRAW ROSIE RACING ACROSS THE SKY SHOOTING HER CANNON!

MOTHER
(ZAGG'S ELEMENTAL BEAM DEPLOYER EBD)

Her shape is what you would expect from a space warrior's weapon: funny-looking. The kind of thing you would see in old sci-fi movies and cartoons.

The grip of a pistol, a bubble shaped barrel with rings around it, a little antennae sticking out from the end, you know what I mean. It looks like your favorite space toy.

Three settings are on the handle:

Freeze Ray (Ice)
Plasma Ray (Fire)
Electro Ray (Electricity)

He calls her Mother because he loves her so much. She's always there when he needs her most. Don't worry, Zagg never kills, but woe to those who don't take Mother seriously!

Brr!
Yowch!
Zap!

DRAW A LARGE DETAILED PICTURE OF MOTHER!

DR. ZENITH'S EVIL ROBOT!

With a gleam in his eye and a terrible grin,
Zenith claps his hands and rubs his chin.
"One more twist, and a few more wires,
And I'll be finished! I'll make them all liars!
They said I couldn't do it, I was crazy, too dumb,
But now they will fear my genius outcome!"
He flips the last switch and turns the last dial,
His eyes open wide and he cracks a dark smile.
The dinosaur before him rattles and shakes,
A shriek and a roar are the first sounds it makes.
Its eyes glow red and its metal teeth shine bright,
Its tail wags slowly and its claws clench tight.
"Yes!" he screams as he looks at his creation,
I'll conquer the city, the Defenders, this nation!
I'll rise to the top. I'll stand on their necks.
In the end all will bow to my Robo-Rex!
The President's daughter, I'll kidnap her quick,
I'll hold her for ransom! Oh my, what a trick!
Dr. Zenith has spoken! There's no time to relax!
I've set things in motion! I will conquer Zorax!"

DRAW A PICTURE OF ROBO-REX ROARING!

THE ABDUCTION OF DAPHNE

She sits in her room looking out over her father's beloved city. Neon lights from the stores and restaurants below shine blinking colors over her purple skin, and turn her silver hair into a rainbow.

She stands from her bed and walks slowly to the window that separates her from the night sky. She presses her hand against the cool glass and looks up. The glow of the city wipes out the stars. She takes a deep breath and sighs.

Being the President's daughter is a complicated thing. It is wonderful at times, but not always. Her father's bodyguards watch her every move, and she often wonders why. Her father is a great man and a great leader. He commands the greatest military force in the Universe, but nothing ever happens in Capitol City. She is treated like a priceless painting hanging in a museum, always being looked at, always kept safe, but never truly free.

She will not complain; she loves her father and will play her part. "A happy daughter means a happy city," he would say to her. Still, to see the stars, to feel the excitement of an adventure...

DRAW DAPHNE STARING AT THE SKY FROM HER TOWER!

BOOM.

She turns her head down to the wide street below. It stretches farther than she can see.

BOOM.

She squints her eyes. Something is moving from far away, something huge, and it is getting closer.

BOOM.

An explosion erupts orange and red flames from the street. A horrible metallic roar rattles the window and she pulls her hand back as if burned.

BOOM.

The behemoth is in view now and she cannot believe what she is seeing. A robot dinosaur, as tall as the tower she lives in, is stomping down Capitol Avenue. Lasers shoot from its eyes destroying the hover vehicles parked along the street. People are running and screaming. Its feet crush the road beneath it and its tail swings heavily into buildings, raining stone and glass onto the sidewalks.

BOOM.

The door to her room implodes and her father's bodyguards run to the window next to her. They look down Capitol Avenue from behind their thick black sunglasses.

"What is it?" she asks them.

The two guards look at each other. "I'm not sure Ms. Daphne but we should be safe in here. This building is stronger than most, and this glass is impenetrable."

"Are you sure?"

"Not to worry, Ms. Daphne, the Planetary Defenders will be here soon. They'll keep us safe."

Daphne relaxes when she hears this, but the monster gets closer. She can see the rows of sharp teeth now and feel the rumble of its steps. She is scared, but she watches its approach.

BOOM.

It is three streets away.

BOOM.

It is two streets away.

BOOM.

The guards look at each other.

BOOM!

Terrible red eyes stare at her through the glass. She wonders how anything can be so big. She screams as a huge claw hits the window and drags its sharp talons along the glass. The force knocks her and the bodyguards to the floor, but the window stands strong.

"See, Ms. Daphne, we told you. You are safe in here."

Daphne stands but she is not so sure she believes them. She notices the big bodyguards are tense. Their hands are on their weapons. She watches the dinosaur open its enormous mouth. The barrel of a strange looking cannon emerges from between its sword-like teeth.

She grabs her head and covers her ears as a high pitched pulsating noise fills her room.

"Sonic disruptor!" yells one of the bodyguards. "Get out of here!"

They scramble to get up. They cover Daphne from behind as they push her towards the door.

Suddenly the window explodes, knocking them to the ground and covering them in large chunks of glass. One piece cuts her cheek.

"Run Ms. Daphne!"

The two guards draw their weapons and start to fire at the face of the dinosaur that fills the space where the window once stood. Their lasers bounce harmlessly off its metallic skin.

The monster reaches a claw into the room, swiping the men into the wall. They crumble into a heap on top of each other.

The mouth opens again and a man stands behind the lower teeth. He is bald and white as snow. A pair of round black glasses cover his eyes and he wears a long white lab coat that buttons from the tops of his shoes up to his chin. He smiles devilishly as he points a strange looking device at her and fires.

DRAW ROBO-REX STARING AT DAPHNE THROUGH THE WINDOW!

Daphne is frozen, trapped in his Paralyzer Beam. She cannot move.

The man steps through the broken window. His boots crunch over the glass as he approaches her. He grabs her chin roughly and stares into her eyes. She can smell the rubber of his black gloves. She is terrified.

"Hello my beauty! Come with me won't you?"

He laughs as he pulls her towards the mouth of Robo-Rex. The Paralyzer Beam still holds her fast. There is nothing she can do to fight back. She cannot even scream.

Robo-Rex swallows her down.

DRAW A PICTURE OF DR. ZENITH & HIS PARALYZER BEAM

FALL OF THE PLANETARY DEFENDERS

They sang their songs.

It roared in rage.

They marched into battle.

It began its rampage.

They fired their plasma beams.

It shot laser eyes.

They brought in their tanks.

It crushed them like flies.

They hit it with bombs.

It spewed fire breath.

They ran for cover.

It scared them to death.

Is this the end, should they raise the white flag?

They hold a little longer, just waiting for Zagg.

DRAW A PICTURE OF ROBO-REX DESTROYING THE TANKS!

ZAGG TO THE RESCUE

In the desert of Zulu,
hidden in the green sand dunes,
is a secret cave lit up by two moons.

Within its rocky walls,
lives a pilot and his ship.
A knight, his horse, and Mother on his hip.

The monitor turns on,
and Zagg gives it a gander.
A face fills the screen, it's Sergeant Null, his Commander.

"We need your help or all is lost,
It's a catastrophe a tragedy with the highest cost!
The President's daughter, has been taken,

the will of our leader has been shaken!
Capitol City is in terrible danger,
will you stop this evil stranger?"

Zagg stares at the screen,
With his one good eye,
"I'm on my way," his only reply.

DRAW CAPTAIN NULL TALKING TO ZAGG ON A BIG SCREEN!

He walks to Rosie,
And opens her dome,
The mission is clear, get the girl home.

Rosie lifts off,
with a rumble and scream.
They rip across the desert, she flies like a dream.

He sees the Defenders,
and they see him.
They cheer and wave, their hope less dim.

He turns his ship,
and she arcs through the sky.
His heart beats steady, there's steel in his eye.

Robo-Rex is ahead,
and it's a murderous sight,
but Zagg and Rosie are prepared for this fight.

It fires its lasers,
but Rosie is quick.
She spins and dodges with a twist and a flick.

It fires again,
this time too fast,
and Rosie is struck by its fiery blast.

She starts to go down,
but one last shot,
"Fire, Rosie! Give it all you got!"

DRAW A PICTURE OF ROSIE BATTLING ROBO-REX!

She fires her cannon,
Her aim is true,
It hits the beast and it splits in two.

Rex falls to the ground,
and Zagg hits eject.
He watches in horror, his little ship wrecked.

Zagg lands on the street,
and he looks to the east.
Dr. Zenith stands there, on what's left of the beast.

He holds the girl,
she can barely stand,
and Mother appears in Zagg's steady hand.

"The Defenders are beaten,
your ship is in flames,
Put down your deployer, enough of your games!"

Zagg is stuck,
His brain racing to think,
And that is when Daphne throws him a wink.

She comes to life,
And bites down on doc's wrist,
He yells out in pain, she escapes with a twist.

"Let's do it for Rosie,"
He whispers to Mother.
He fires a freeze ray, then fires another.

DRAW DAPHNE ESCAPING AND ZAGG FREEZING DR. ZENITH!

Dr. Zenith is frozen,
And Daphne is free,
The President arrives and he falls to one knee.

"Thank you dear Zagg,
you saved her life.
You've saved us all from this terrible strife.

What can I do?
What price can I pay?
Anything you want! What do you say?"

"I ask one thing,
and I think that it's fair.
My ship is in need of a major repair.

When Rosie is back,
and evil stands tall,
Just give us a ring. We'll answer the call."

DRAW A PICTURE OF ZAGG TALKING TO PRESIDENT ZANTHOS

THE END

President Zanthos did, indeed, fix Rosie. She sat there gleaming in the sun at the end of the parade route. Zagg stood next to her, in his most decorated uniform. It felt tight on his neck as he stood at attention. Rows upon rows of Planetary Defenders marched passed him saluting the pilot who saved them, once again, from Evil's deadly embrace.

The cheers of Capitol City's citizens echoed for miles and confetti swirled through the air like a blizzard as a band played the Zorax national anthem <u>O'er The Green Dunes</u>.

President Zanthos made a short speech that whipped the crowd into a frenzy. His smile was so wide and bright, the crowd could see it from three blocks away. He swept his arm to the left in a grand gesture as Daphne walked toward the podium.

Zagg could not help but look at her. In fact the whole city hushed as she neared him. She was dressed in a gown of dazzling silver, the same color as her hair. It seemed to dance over her lithe frame as her long strides closed the distance to her hero.

She held a small box and stopped directly in front of him. She opened the box and produced a large gold medal. She held it up to the crowd but the silence only grew. Zagg straightened as she pinned the medal to his chest. She put her small hands on his shoulders and kissed his cheek. His skin burned under her touch and a small smile cracked his stoic countenance.

"Thank you Captain Zagg," she said.

"We did it together," he replied.

She threw him the same wink she gave before biting Dr. Zenith's wrist. Then she turned away and presented him to the city.

The roar of the crowd was deafening.

The parade was talked about for months afterward, but Zagg heard none of it. Zagg does not fight for glory or riches. He fights to defend what is good and just.

Zagg returned to his cave with his newly repaired Rosie. And there they wait. Until next time.

USE BOTH PAGES TO DRAW ZAGG RECEIVING HIS MEDAL

RESOURCES

Dear Reader:

This is just the beginning. You can find out more about drawing, illustrating stories, writing your own stories, keeping a journal or sketch book, and much more!

Visit your local library and ask your librarians for help. They might recommend the DRAW RIGHT NOW series by Marie Hablitzel and Kim Stitzer, ART FOR KIDS: DRAWING by Kathryn Temple, THE DRAWING BOOK FOR KIDS: 365 DAILY THINGS TO DRAW (a Woo! Jr. Kids Activities Book), or the KID'S GUIDE TO DRAWING books by Laura Murawski.

When you're on the internet, you could visit Activity Village for its Learn to Draw tutorials (www.activityvillage.co.uk/learn-to-draw), find out "How to Draw" on Art Projects for Kids (artprojectsforkids.org), or sign up for Drawing Bootcamp on www.jam.com.

But my favorite thing to do is visit YouTube which has a lot of really fun how-to videos, like:

- DrawKidsDraw (www.youtube.com/drawkidsdraw)
- Art for Kids Hub (www.youtube.com/ArtforKidsHub)
- Art Time with Mr. Mayberry (www.youtube.com, then search for Art time with Mr. Mayberry
- Robot Art School (www.youtube.com, then search for Robot Art School)

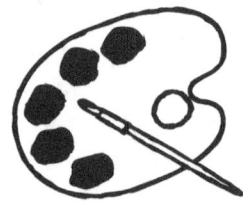 If you need inspiration for your drawings, you might want to learn about famous artists and their artwork on websites like WikiArt (www.wikiart) and on museum websites. Visit the National Gallery of Art in Washington, D.C. or the Metropolitan Museum of Art in New York City websites, for example. You can also look for books like A CHILD'S INTRODUCTION TO ART: THE WORLD'S GREATEST PAINTINGS AND SCULPTURES by Heather Alexander and Meredith Hamilton, that introduce readers to many artists and types of art.

Can you tell I'm excited about helping you learn to draw? To help you explore drawing and art more, I've added these Resources to the Spowerks Storyboard website. Just look for the Resources tab at www.spowerks.com for more ways you can explore your own imagination!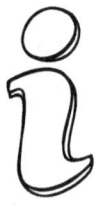

Sincerely,

C.S. Moon, Author

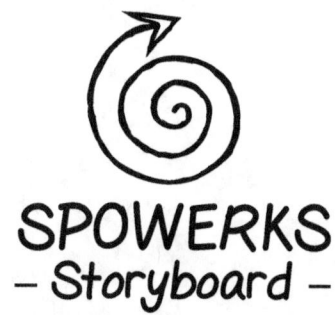

SPOWERKS
– Storyboard –

HELPING KIDS EXPLORE IMAGINATION THROUGH STORYTELLING & ART

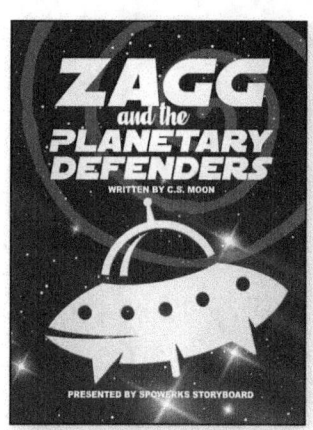

ZAGG & THE PLANETARY DEFENDERS
by C.S. Moon
48 Pages, 8.5 x 11, $12.99
ISBN: 78-1-73256170-0

Meet Zagg, a heroic pilot who lives on the planet Zorax. Together with the Planetary Defenders, he must stop the evil Dr. Zenith and his powerful robot dinosaur! Prose and poetry combine in this story for kids ages 9-12. But while the story is written, you create the illustrations! That's right, there are a lot of blank pages in this book. We want you to use your imagination to create the pictures for Zagg and his companions!

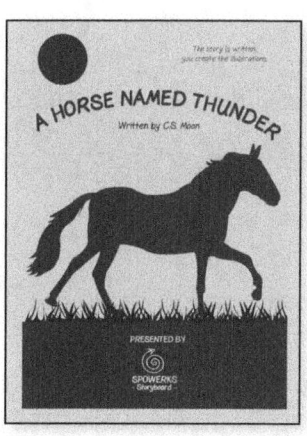

A HORSE NAMED THUNDER
by C.S. Moon
50 Pages, 8.5 x 11, $12.99
ISBN: 978-0-692-88018-0

For kids ages 9-12. Within these pages is a story of a horse with big dreams and a big heart. But while the story is written, you create the illustrations! That's right, there are a lot of blank pages in this book. We want you to use your imagination to create the pictures for A HORSE NAMED THUNDER! It's fun and creative, and in the end, you get to add your name as the illustrator!

For more information, resources, and to order books, please visit:

www.spowerks.com
SPOWERKS • P.O. Box 23 • Columbia, CT 06237

www.ingramcontent.com/pod-product-compliance
Lightning Source LLC
Chambersburg PA
CBHW062342220526
45469CB00008B/2811